HISTORICAL NOTES

OF THE FAMILY OF

KIP of KIPSBURG and KIP'S BAY,

NEW YORK.

PRIVATELY PRINTED.

1871.

Windham Press is committed to bringing the lost cultural heritage of ages past into the 21st century through high-quality reproductions of original, classic printed works at affordable prices.

This book has been carefully crafted to utilize the original images of antique books rather than error-prone OCR text. This also preserves the work of the original typesetters of these classics, unknown craftsmen who laid out the text, often by hand, of each and every page you will read. Their subtle art involving judgment and interaction with the text is in many ways superior and more human than the mechanical methods utilized today, and gave each book a unique, hand-crafted feel in its text that connected the reader organically to the art of bindery and book-making.

We think these benefits are worth the occasional imperfection resulting from the age of these books at the time of scanning, and their vintage feel provides a connection to the past that goes beyond the mere words of the text.

As bibliophiles, we are always seeking perfection in our work, so please notify us of any errors in this book by emailing us at corrections@windhampress.com. Our team is motivated to correct errors quickly so future customers are better served. Our mission is to raise the bar of quality for reprinted works by a focus on detail and quality over mass production.

To peruse our catalog of carefully curated classic works, please visit our online store at www.windhampress.com.

WINDHAM PRESS
CLASSIC REPRINTS

ALBANY:
JOEL MUNSELL.
1871.

"It is wise for us to recur to the history of our ancestors. Those who are regardless of their ancestors and their posterity, who do not look upon themselves as a link connecting the past with the future in the transmission of life from their ancestors to their posterity, do not perform their duty to the world. To be faithful to ourselves we must keep our ancestors and posterity within reach and grasp of our thoughts and affections, living in the memory and retrospect of the past, and hoping with affection and care for those who are to come after us. We are true to ourselves only when we act with becoming pride for the blood we inherit, and which we are to transmit to those who shall soon fill our places."........DANIEL WEBSTER.

ARMS.

The earliest copy, in this country, of the arms of the family, was found in the first Dutch Church erected in New York about 1640. This Church was built by a number of the Dutch families, of which this was one, and their arms were pictured on the stained glass windows. They were also carved in stone over the door of the Kip's Bay House, which was erected in 1655.

HISTORY AND PEDIGREE.

The DE KYPE family was originally settled for a long period near Alençon in Bretagne. The first of whom there is any notice in history is:

I. RULOFF DE KYPE. In the sixteenth century, he was a warm adherent of the Guises, and took prominent part, in that section of country, in the civil war between the Catholics and Protestants. On the triumph of the Protestants, under Conde, in 1562, his chateau was taken and burned, and he was forced to fly. He took refuge in the Low Countries with his three sons, where they lived for several years under an assumed name. In 1569, with his son Henri, he reentered France, joined the army of the Duke of Anjou, and on the 13th of March, fell in the battle fought on the banks of La Charante, near Jarnac.[1] By the care of his son, Jean Baptiste, who was a priest, he was buried in a small church in the neighborhood of

---

[1] *Duyckinck's Encyclopedia of American Literature*, vol. II, p. 551.

Jarnac, where an altar tomb was erected to his memory, which was destroyed with the church during the French revolution, at the close of the last century. The inscription on the tomb mentioned him as RULOFF DE KYPE, ECUYER,[1] and was surmounted by his arms,[2] with two crests, one a game cock, the other a demi-griffin holding a cross, both of which crests have been used by different branches of the family in this country. He left issue:

1. HENRI, who, after his father's death, entered the army of one of the Italian princes, where he spent his life. He *d. unm.*
2. JEAN BAPTISTE, priest in the Church of Rome.
3. RULOFF, of whom, next following.

II. RULOFF had remained in the Low Countries, where he became a Protestant and settled at Amsterdam. He seems to have dropped from his name the French prefix De. He was born in 1544 and died in 1596, leaving issue:

Hendrick, of whom next following.

III. HENDRICK (in Eng. Henry), *b.* in 1576. We copy the following account of him from Duyckinck:[3] "On arriv-

---

[1] This title designates a gentleman who had a right to coat armor.
[2] *Lossing's Field Book of the Revolution,* vol. I, p. 803.
[3] *Encyclopedia of American Literature,* vol. II, p 551. See, also *Holgate's Genealogies,* p. 8, 9, 109.

ing at manhood he took an active part in the 'Company of Foreign Countries,' an association formed for the purpose of obtaining access to the Indies, by a different route from that pursued by Spain and Portugal. They first attempted to sail round the northern seas of Europe and Asia; but their expedition, dispatched in 1594, was obliged to return on account of the ice, in the same year. In 1609, they employed Henry Hudson to sail to the westward, in the little Half Moon, with happier results.

Henry Kype came to New Amsterdam in 1635. He returned to Holland, but his sons remained, and rose to important positions as citizens and landed proprietors."

He *m.* Margaret de Marneil, and had issue:

1. Hendrick. His name is frequently mentioned in the early records of the Colony. The first application for a municipal form of government, made to "The Lords' States General of the United Netherlands." July 26, 1649, was signed by eleven of the leading citizens, of whom he was one.[1]

    In 1647 he was appointed one of the Council of "Nine Men," who were to assist the Governor.[2]

    He *m.* Anna, daughter of the Hon. Nicasius De Sille, First Counsellor to the Director General Peter Stuyvesant.[3] She *d.* Feb. 29, 1660.

---

[1] *Brodhead's History of State of New York*, vol. I, p. 505.

[2] *O'Callaghan's History of New Netherland*, vol. II, p. 37.

[3] For account of De Sille, see *O'Callaghan*, II, 236, *note*.

2. Jacobus. (In Eng. James). Born May 15, 1631. He was appointed Secretary of the Council of the colony in 1653. In
1659, he was elected *schepen* (alderman), of New Amsterdam, and filled that office also in 1662, '63, '65, '73 and '74.[1]
He obtained a grant from the government of the property
on the East river which was known as the Kip's Bay Farm,
and where in 1655 he erected, what, for the next two centuries, was the family residence.[2]

He *m.* Maria, daughter of the Hon. Johannes de la Montaigne, a Huguenot, who was associated with Gov. Kieft in
the government of the colony. She was *b.* at sea, off the
island of Madeira, Jan. 26, 1637, and *m.* in the fort at New
Amsterdam, Feb. 14, 1654, in her 17th year.[3]

3. Isaac. Of whom, next following.

IV. Isaac. He had large landed property in the city,
including what now forms the Park. Nassau street was
then called Kip street, in honor of him, and is so laid down
in the early maps.[4]

In 1657, " in conformity to the laudable custom of the
city of Amsterdam in Europe," the Great Burgher Right
was introduced into New Amsterdam, by Gov. Stuyvesant.
It was the selection of about twenty families who formed
the Great Citizenship, the members of which alone were

---

[1] *O'Callaghan*, II, 213, *note.*

[2] For an historical account of this place see *Appendix* I.

[3] *Holgate*, p. 112.   [4] *Ibid.*

eligible to the public offices, while the rest of the citizens were in the Small Citizenship. In the list of the Great Citizenship are found the names of Hendrick and Isaac Kip.[1] "These twenty names," says Stone — "composed the aristocracy of New York two hundred and nine years ago...... In a few short years it was found that this division of the citizens into two classes produced great inconvenience in consequence of the very small number of Great Burghers who were eligible to office. In the year 1668, the difference between ' great ' and ' small ' burghers was absolutely abolished"[2]

He *m.* Feb. 8, 1653, Catalina de Suyers, by whom he had issue : —

1. Hendrick, *b.* 1654, *m.* 1697, Magdalene Van Kleek.
2. Cornelia, *b.* 1656.
3. Abraham, *b.* 1659, *m.* 1697, Catalina de la Noy.
4. Isaac, *b.* 1662, *m.* Oct. 3, 1686, Sarah de Mill.
5. Jacobus, of whom presently.

Johannes

He married, second, Sept. 18, 1675, Mrs. Maria Vermilye, widow of Johannes de la Montaigne, Jr.,[3] by whom he left no issue.

---

[1] *Paulding's Affairs and Men of New Amsterdam*, p. 87.
[2] *History of New York City*, by Wm. L. Stone, 1866, p. 33.
[3] See *O'Callaghan's History*, II, p. 21, *note*.

V. JACOBUS, *b.* Aug. 25, 1666. He, with his brother Hendrick, were the co-patentees of the Manor of Kipsburg. Of this, Holgate gives the following account: "In the following generation, we find the family purchasing from the Esopus Indians, on the east side of the Hudson river, where Rhinebeck now stands, a tract of land extending four miles along the river and several miles inland. The original deed, which is still preserved, is dated July 28, 1686, and signed by three Indian chiefs, *Ankony, Anamaton* and *Collicoon.* Two years afterwards, a Royal Patent, dated June 2, 1688, was granted by His Excellency, Thomas Dongan, Governor of the Province of New York, under the name of the Manor of Kipsburg, in confirmation of the Indian title. One-fifth part of this manor was afterwards sold to Col. Henry Beekman, through whose granddaughter, the mother of Chancellor Livingston, it passed into the Livingston family." [1]

In this generation the spelling of the family name seems to have been fixed. On first coming to the country, it was KYPE, being so signed by Hendrick KYPE to public documents in 1643.[2] Holgate thus traces the change: "After the conquest of New Netherland by the English, the name was anglicized to KIP. See Royal Charter

---

[1] *Holgate's Genealogies,* p. 110.   [2] See *O'Callaghan's History,* I, 284.

granted by Gov. Dongan in 1686, and that of Gov. Montgomerie in 1730, where members of the family are mentioned as officers under the crown, and where the name is anglicised to KIP, which fixed its spelling."[1]

He *m.* first, May 29, 1685, Mrs. Henrietta Wessels, widow of the Hon. Gulian Verplanck of Verplanck's point, by whom he had no children; and secondly, in 1695, Rachel daughter of John Swarthout, Esq., *b.* April 10, 1669, and *d.* Sept. 16, 1717. He *d.* Feb. 28, 1753, leaving issue : —

1. ISAAC, of whom presently.
2. Roeloff, of Kipsburgh, from whom that branch of the family descended. He died during the Revolution, aged 90 years.

VI. ISAAC, *b.* Jan. 8, 1696, *m.* Jan. 7, 1720, Cornelia, daughter of Leonard Lewis, Esq., alderman of New York, 1696–1700.[2] She was *b.* Nov. 9, 1692, and *d.* July 10, 1772. He *d.* July 2, 1762, leaving issue : —

1. Elizabeth, *b.* 1721, *d. unm.*
2. LEONARD, of whom presently.
3. Rachel, *b.* 1725.
4. Isaac, *b.* 1732, physician, *m.* Rachel, daughter of Jacob Kip, Esq., of Kipsburg.
5. Abraham, *m.* 1767, Dorothea Remsen.
6. Jacobus, *m.* 1753, Elizabeth Frazier, and left issue : —

---

[1] *Holgate's Genealogies*, p. 109. [2] *Ibid.*, p. 112.

Samuel, Captain of Dragoons in British army. Of him Bolton gives the following account: "The command of the Loyalist Rangers afforded Col. De Lancey, facilities for communicating with his old associates in this section of the country, and was the means of inducing some of the landed gentry to take an active part in the contest. This was particularly the case with Samuel Kip, Esq., of a family which from the first settlement of the country by the Dutch had possessed a grant of land at Kip's Bay, and in other parts of New York island. Having been always associated with the government, and from their landed interest wielding an influence in its affairs, they were naturally disposed to espouse the royal cause. In addition to this, Mr. Kip's estate was near Col. Delancey's, and a close intimacy had always existed between them. He was, therefore, easily induced to accept a Captain's commission from the royal government and embark all his interests in this contest. He raised a company of cavalry, principally from his own tenants, joined the British army with the Colonel, and from his intimate knowledge of the country, was enabled to gain the reputation of an active and daring partisan officer. For this reason he was for a time assigned to a command in the Loyalist Rangers. In one of the severe skirmishes which took place in Westchester county in 1781, Captain Kip, while charging a body of American troops, had his horse killed under him, and received a severe bayonet wound. He survived, however, several years after the war, though like his friend Delancey, a heavy pecuniary sufferer from the cause he had espoused."[1]

---

[1] *Bolton's History of Westchester*, vol. II, p. 254   An account of this fight in Westchester, is given by Gen. Heath in his *Memorabilia*, p. 324, though

VII. Leonard, *b.* 1725. He was a loyalist during the revolution, and though incapacitated by ill health from taking any active part in the contest, yet his principles were well known; and several of the family being in the British army, during his absence from the city, the greater part of his property was confiscated.

He *m.* April 11, 1763, Elizabeth, daughter of Francis Marschalk, Esq., of New York. She was *b.* 1732 and *d.* 1818. He *d.* 1804, leaving issue: —

1. Anne, *b.* 1764, *d. unm.*, 1796.
2. Isaac Lewis, *b.* 1767. He was the law partner of Judge Brockholdst Livingston, and was appointed by Chancellor Livingston, Register of the Court of Chancery, which responsible office he held under Chancellors Livingston, Lansing, and Kent, and finally relinquished it by his own voluntary choice.

   He *m.* Sarah, daughter of Jer. Smith, Esq., of Elizabethtown, New Jersey, who *d.* 1843. He *d.* 1837, leaving issue: —

   i. Brockholdst Livingston, *d unm.*
   ii. Leonard Wm., *m.* Anna Corbet, daughter of William Wilson, Esq. of New York, *d.* May 15, 1863.

---

he makes the mistake of saying, that Capt. Kip was mortally wounded. Bolton says: "A full narrative of this memorable event has been published in almost every country in Europe, showing what a handful of infantry could do, opposed to a strong force of horse."— *History of Westchester*, vol. I, p. 260.

iii. Francis Marschalk. D.D., pastor of the Dutch church,
Fishkill, New York. He *m*. Mary, daughter of John
R. Bayard. Esq., of New York.

3. LEONARD, of whom, next following.

VIII. LEONARD, *b*. 1774, *d*. July 2, 1846. We copy the
following obituary notice, published at the time of his
death: "We notice in our paper the announcement of
the death of Leonard Kip, Esq., and although there are few
now remaining who were his cotemporaries, we cannot
permit one of our most estimable citizens thus to pass
away, without at least a brief notice.

Mr. Kip was a member of one of our oldest New York
families, which more than two centuries ago, obtained a
grant on the island of the property afterwards known by the
name of the Kip's Bay Estate. For the next hundred
years, in connection with the Stuyvesants, Beekmans, De-
lanceys, Depeysters, and other Dutch and Huguenot
families, they exerted a controlling influence in the colony.

*   *   *   *   *   *   *   *   *

At the time of his death Mr. Kip must have been several years past seventy. When preparing to enter on active
life, he found that during the political convulsions of the
Revolution, much of his family property had been swept
away; and after an unsuccessful law suit for its recovery,

in which Alexander Hamilton was his counsel, he abandoned all further attempts for fear of hazarding what remained. He therefore turned to commerce and was enabled by skill and prudence to repair his shattered fortunes. He then withdrew from business, leaving behind him an enviable reputation for ability and integrity, and shortly afterwards accepted the office of President of the North River Bank, an office which he held from the first chartering of that institution, until within the last five years. Being then induced by his failing health to leave the city, he withdrew to the neighborhood of Hartford, Connecticut, where he spent the remainder of his days.

It is, however, particularly in connection with many whose names formerly stood high in the political history of our city, that we remember the subject of this notice. For himself he sought nothing from politics. At the close of the last war, in 1814, he was, for a few years, a member of the Common Council of our city; but he soon withdrew, and ever afterwards declined a nomination to any office. There was, however, in those days, a coterie of gentlemen in our city, with whom he was linked from social feelings. Clinton, Radcliff, Duane, Colden, D. D. Tompkins, Brockholdst Livingston, the Swarthouts, Morrises and others, formed a circle which for elegance and high-toned honor will not soon be seen again. Perhaps the liability which then existed, of being held personally answerable for their words, false as the principle may have been, produced a courtesy not known in these days. Many of these gentlemen we have mentioned, were obliged practically to exhibit this; and some of our old citizens will still remember the sensation produced by the duel between Clinton and Swarthout, and the fatal combats between Judge Livingston and Jones, and young Hamilton and Eckard.

With these men we were accustomed to see Mr. Kip; and although he differed widely from some of them in politics, for he was a 'high-toned Federalist,' even in the warmest party times, he seemed to preserve his social feelings unchanged. With the Vice-President, D. D. Tompkins, there had been a friendship since their boyhood, which remained unbroken till Mr. T.'s death. We remember, on one occasion, thirty years ago, when we met Mr. Kip at his table, hearing them, as they referred to their early adventures. laugh over the wide distance which had since separated them in politics.

These men have now all gone, and the few who remember them must soon follow. Yet among the last generation we know none who for uprightness and high honorable principles, exceeded the subject of this brief notice, and we cannot forbear, therefore, paying his memory this last tribute."[1]

He *m.* Dec. 12, 1809, Maria, daughter of Duncan Ingraham, Esq., of Greenvale Farm,[2] near Poughkeepsie, New York, and left issue :

1. WM. INGRAHAM, of whom presently.
2. Elizabeth, *m* Oct. 26, 1836, Rev. Henry L. Storrs, rector of St. John's church, Yonkers, New York (son of Hon. Henry R. Storrs, M. C., from Utica, N. Y.). He *d.* May 16, 1852, leaving issue.

    i.   Eliza, *d. unm.*
    ii. Maria.
    iii. Leonard Kip, in Holy Orders, rector of St. Stephen's Church, Pittsfield, Mass.

3. Sophia, *m.* Oct. 26, 1846, the Right Rev. George Burgess, D.D., Bishop of Maine. He *d.* April 23, 1816, leaving issue :

    Mary Georgiana.

4. Mary, *m.* Jan. 27, 1848, John Innes Kane, Esq., of Woodlawn, Westchester Co., New York (son of Oliver Kane, Esq., of New York), who *d.* at Palermo, Sicily, Dec. 21, 1851. She *d.* May 12, 1852, leaving issue :

    John Innes, *b.* Nov. 13, 1849.

5. Leonard, *m.* Oct. 26, 1852, Harriet Letitia, daughter of Hon. John S. Van Rensselaer of Albany, N. Y.[3]

---

[1] *New York Commercial Advertiser*, July, 1846.
[2] See *Ingraham Family* in Appendix.
[3] See *Van Rensselaer Family* in Appendix.

IX. RIGHT REV. WM. INGRAHAM, KIP, D.D., Bishop of California.

Ordained Deacon July 1, 1835, and Priest in the following November. Successively, Rector of St. Peter's Church, Morristown, New Jersey, Assistant Minister of Grace Church, New York and Rector of St. Paul's Church, Albany, New York.

Elected Missionary Bishop of California by the House of Bishops, Oct. 28, 1853, and Diocesan Bishop by the Convention of the Protestant Episcopal Church in California, April, 1857.

Author of *Lenten Fast, Double Witness of the Church, Christmas Holidays in Rome, Early Conflicts of Christianity, Catacombs of Rome, Early Jesuit Missions in North America, Unnoticed Things of Scripture*, etc., etc.

He m. July 1, 1835, Maria Elizabeth, daughter of Isaac Lawrence, Esq., of New York,[1] and has issue: —

1. LAWRENCE, of whom presently.
2. Wm. Ingraham, b. Jan. 15, 1840, Secretary of the United States Legation to Japan, 1861–2.

    He m. Feb. 28, 1865, in the English Chapel, Nice, France, Elizabeth Clementina, daughter of Hon. Wm. B. Kinney,

---

[1] See *Lawrence Family* in Appendix.

formerly Minister of the United States to the Court of Turin, and has issue : —

Wm. Ingraham, *b.* Jan. 13, 1867.

Lawrence, *b.* Oct. 2, 1869.

X. LAWRENCE, *b.* Sept. 17, 1836. Brevet Lieutenant Colonel in the Third Artillery, United States Army.

Appointed Cadet at Westpoint, June, 1853. 2d Lieut. Third Artillery, June, 1857, and was at once employed in the expedition, under General Wright, against the Northern Indians, where he acted as Adjutant of the Artillery Battalion, and distinguished himself in the battles of Four Lakes and Spokan Plains. He published an account of the campaign in a volume entitled *Army Life on the Pacific.*

At the opening of the civil war, in 1861, he was Adjutant of the Third Artillery, which place he resigned to go upon General Sumner's Staff, as senior Aid-de-camp, with the rank of Major. He was engaged with the Army of the Potomac, in the battles of Yorktown, Williamsburg, Fair Oaks, Seven Pines, Allen's Farm, Savage's Station, Glendale, Malvern Hill, Antietam, Fredericksburg, Mine Run, etc.

During the Seven Days' Battles, in front of Richmond, he was acting Adjutant General of Sumner's corps, and was recommended by him to the War Department, for brevet Captain and brevet Major, " for gallantry in the Seven Days' Battles." But none of the recommendations with regard to General McClellan's campaign were acted on by the Senate.

After the death of General Sumner, he was attached to the Staff of General Wool, and assigned to duty at the Head Quarters of the Department of the East, as Assistant Inspector General of Artillery. Six months afterwards he was ordered to again join the Army of the Potomac, and was assigned to duty on the Staff of Brevet Major General R. O. Tyler, as Inspector of the Artillery Reserve, and took part in the battle of Rappahanock Station, etc.

When the Reserve was broken up, he was appointed Aid-de-camp on the Staff of Major General Sheridan, and was engaged in the following battles: Trevillian Station (where he was wounded), Dinwiddie Court House, Cedar Creek, "Sheridan's Ride," (where he was again slightly wounded), High Bridge, Five Forks, Sailor's Creek, Appomattox Station, and Appomattox Court House, where General Lee surrendered.

He was appointed *Captain by brevet*, June 11, 1864, " for gallant and meritorious service at the battle of Trevillian Station, Va. ;" *Major by brevet*, March 31, 1865, " for gallant and meritorious service in the Cavalry campaign from Winchester to Petersburg and at the battle of Dinwiddie Court House, Va. ;" *Lieutenant Colonel by brevet*, April 1, 1865, " for gallant and meritorious service at the battle of Five Forks, Va."

General Sheridan, in his official dispatch to the War Department, says : " Major Kip has been acting as Aid-de-camp to me since June, 1864, and during that time has taken an active part, as such, in all the campaigns, battles, etc., in which I have been engaged. He is a most brave and gallant officer, possessed of fine intelligence and gentlemanly demeanor. I desire to retain him on my personal Staff, and consider that the promotion is only due him for past faithful and invaluable services."

While on the Staff of General Wool, he was appointed by Gov. Horatio Seymour of New York, Lieutenant Colonel of the Eighth New York regiment of Heavy Artillery, but the War Department was unwilling to relieve him from present duties to allow him to accept.

He m. April 23, 1867, Eva, daughter of Peter Lorillard, Esq., of New York, and has had issue : —

> Eva Maria, who d. Feb. 9, 1870.
> Edith.

APPENDIX.

I.

The Kip's Bay House.

4

THE KIP'S BAY HOUSE.

Though many years have passed since this place was swept away by the encroachments of the city, yet it exists among the recollection of the writer's earliest days, when it was looked upon as the first home of the family on this continent. It was erected in 1655 by Jacobus Kip, Secretary of the Council, who received a grant of that part of the island. The bricks of which it was built were imported from Holland. Parts of it were rebuilt in 1696.

There is, in the collection of the Bishop of California, a picture of it as it appeared at the time of the Revolution. It was a large double house, with three windows in a row on one side of the door and two on the other, with one large wing. On the right hand of the hall was the dining room, running from front to rear, with two windows looking out over the bay and two over the country on the other side. This was the room which was afterwards invested with interest from its connection with Major André. In the rear was a pear tree planted by the ladies of the family in 1700, which bore fruit until the destruction of the house in 1851. In this residence five generations of the family were born.

Then came the Revolution, and Sargent, in his *Life of André*, thus gives its history in those stirring times. "Where now, in New York, is the unalluring and crowded neighborhood of the Second Avenue and Thirty-Fifth street, stood in 17-0, the ancient *bowerie*, or country seat of Jacobus Kip. Built in 1655 of bricks brought from Holland, encompassed by pleasant trees and in easy view of the sparkling waters of Kip's bay on the East river, the mansion remained even to our own times in possession of one of its founder's line. Here"—[continues Sargent, incorporating the humorous recollections of Irving's *Knickerbocker*,] "spread the same smiling meadows whose appearance had so expanded the heart of Oloffe the dreamer, in the fabulous age of the colony; here, still nodded the groves that had echoed back the thunder of Hendrick Kip's musketoon, when that mighty warrior left his name to the surrounding waves. When Washington was in the neighborhood, Kip's house had been his quarters: when Howe crossed from Long Island, on Sunday, September 15, 1776, he debarked at the rocky point hard by, and his skirmishers drove our people from their position behind the dwelling. Since then, it had known many guests. Howe, Clinton, Kniphausen, Percy, were sheltered by its roof. The aged owner, with his wife and daughters, remained; but they had always an officer of distinction quartered with them; and if a part of the family were in arms for Congress, as is alleged, it is certain that others were active for the Crown." [1]

The Baroness de Riedesel, when with her husband in the British army, was for some time a visitor here.

In 1790 it was held by Colonel Williams of the 80th Royal Regiment, and here on the evening of the 19th of September, he gave a dinner to Sir Henry Clinton and his Staff, as a parting compliment to André. The aged owner of the house was present, and when the Revolution was over, he described the scene and the incidents of that dinner. At the table Sir Henry Clinton announced the departure of André, next morning, on a secret and most important expedition, and added (what the writer has never seen mentioned in any other account and what was probably to have been André's reward): "Plain John André will come back Sir John André."

André, it was said by Mr. Kip, was evidently depressed, and took but little part in the merriment about him; and when, in his turn, it became necessary for him to sing, he gave the favorite military *chanson* attributed to Wolfe,

---

[1] *Life of André*, p. 267.

who sang it on the eve of the battle of Quebec in which he died.

> " Why, soldiers, why,
>   Should we be melancholy, boys?
> Why, soldiers, why,
>   Whose business 'tis to die!
> For should next campaign,
>   Send us to Him who made us, boys,
> We're free from pain :
>   But should we remain,
> A bottle and kind landlady
>   Makes all well again."

His biographer, after copying this account, adds : " How brilliant soever the company, how cheerful the repast, its memory must have been fraught with sadness to both host and guests. It was the last occasion of André's meeting his comrades in life. Four short days gone, the hands then clasped by friendship, were fettered by hostile bonds; yet nine days more, and the darling of the army, the youthful hero of the hour, had dangled from a gibbet."[1]

After the Revolution, the place remained in its owner's possession, for his age had fortunately prevented him from being guilty of any overt act. And when Washington, in the hour of his triumph, returned to New York, he went

---

[1] *Sargent's Life of André*, p. 268.

out to visit again those who in 1776 had been his involun-
tary hosts. Dr. Francis relates an interesting little inci-
dent which occurred at this visit: "On the old road
towards Kingsbridge, on the eastern side of the island,
was the well known Kip's farm, pre-eminently distinguished
for its grateful fruits, the plum, the peach, the pear, and
the apple, and for its choice culture of the *rosaceæ*. Here,
the *elite* often repaired, and here our Washington, now
invested with Presidential honors, made an excursion, and
was presented with the *rosa Gallica*, an exotic first introduced into the country, in this garden; fit emblem of that
memorable union of France and the American colonies,
in the cause of republican freedom."[1]

In 1851, this old place was demolished. It had then
stood a hundred and ninety-six years, and was the oldest
house on the island. It was swallowed up by the growth
of the mighty metropolis, and Thirty-Fifth street runs over
the spot where once stood the old mansion. A short time
before, after it had been deserted, the writer made his last
visit to it, and as he stood in the old dining room, there
came back to him visions of the many noble and chivalrous
men who in the last two centuries had feasted within its

[1] *Old New York*, Anniversary Discourse before the New York Historical
Society, Nov. 17, 1857, by John W. Francis, M.D., LL.D.

walls. Some time afterwards, a gentleman from West-chester wrote him, that happening to pass, he saw they were taking down the building, and he advised the writer to secure the old stone coat of arms, which he saw, over the hall door, projecting from the half demolished walls. But he was engaged at the time and neglected to do so.

APPENDIX.

II.

Families Intermarried.

I.

INGRAHAM.

Genealogists begin the record of this family, with Randolph, the son of Ingel'ram or Ing'ram, who was Sheriff of Nottingham and Derby in the beginning of the reign of Henry II, as were his sons Robert and William. Robert Ingram, Knight, whose arms are painted at Temple Newsam, was of so great eminency in the reign of Henry III, that the Prior and Convent of Lenton granted to him a yearly rent out of their lands in Sheynton and Nottingham for his military services in their defense.

In the reign of James I, Sir Arthur Ingram obtained a grant of Temple Newsam, near Leeds. This, which is still the family seat, had been a Preceptory of the Temple Knights until the expulsion of the order in 1312, when it escheated to the crown, and was granted by Edward III to Sir John Darcy. His descendant, Thomas, Lord Darcy and Meinell, was attainted and beheaded for his part in the rising in the reign of Henry VIII, called the Pilgrimage of Grace, when Temple Newsam became again forfeited to the crown. In 1554, Henry VIII granted it to Matthew, Earl of Lennox, and here was born his son Henry Darnley, the future husband of Mary, Queen of Scotland. The room is still called the the King's Chamber. James I, of England and VI of Scotland, the son of Darnley, gave it to his kinsman, Esme Stuart, Duke of Lennox, from whom it passed to Sir Arthur Ingram, one of the conditions of the sale being, that the room in which Darnley was born should not be altered.

During the great rebellion, the Ingram family were distinguished for their adherence to the cause of their sovereign. One of the family, Sir William Ingram was Groom of the Chambers to Charles II, while Sir Arthur was celebrated for his exertions as a cavalier. He was twice married; first to Eleanor, daughter of Sir Henry Slingsby of the Red House, and second, to the Lady Katherine, daughter of Thomas, Lord Viscount Fairfax of Gilling. When the Parliament triumphed, he probably owed his safety to this relationship to Lord Fairfax, and to the fact that his eldest son had married Anne, daughter of Montacute, Earl of Manchester, also a Parliamentary leader.

Sir Arthur was a near relation of Wentworth, the celebrated Earl of Stafford, many of whose letters are in the library at Temple Newsam.

On the Restoration, six years after the death of Sir Arthur, Charles II, to recompense the loyalty of the family, created his eldest son Henry, a peer of Scotland, under the title of Viscount Irwin, by letters patent, dated May 23, 1661.

The Ingraham family in this country (the spelling of the name having been altered), are descended from the second son of Sir Arthur, Arthur Ingram of Barrowby, who married a daughter of Sir John Mallory. The portraits of Sir Arthur, in cavalier costume, of the first Viscount Irwin, in full armor, and the second Viscount Irwin, in half armor (all nearly full length), are in the collection of the Bishop of California.

The male branch in England, as descended from the first Viscount, became extinct with Charles Ingram, ninth Viscount Irwin, who died in 1778.[1] His daughters, the Marchioness of Hertford and Lady William Gordon successively inherited Temple Newsam, and from them it passed to their sister, Mrs. Hugo Meynell, whose son took the name of Ingram, and his family are now owners of the family estates.

With the younger branch, in this country, the navy seems to have been the favorite profession. Besides many

---

[1] See *Burke's Extinct Peerage.*

others connected with the service, we may mention, Captain Joseph Ingraham, who was lost at sea, in 1799, in command of the Sloop of war *Pickering*; Lieut. Wm. Ingraham, who was killed in 1802, in action with the Indians on the Pacific coast; and in this generation, Commodore Duncan N. Ingraham (of South Carolina), who when commanding the *St. Louis*, in 1853, gained a world wide reputation by his decision in forcing the Austrian vessels of war, in the harbor of Smyrna, to surrender up a prisoner who claimed American citizenship. Four of the name died gallantly in battle during the civil war, three on the Confederate and one on the Federal side.

Duncan Ingraham, Esq., the father of Mrs. LEONARD KIP of New York, was a loyalist during the revolution, and went to Europe in 1776 where he remained until the peace of 1784. He is frequently mentioned by President John Adams, then Minister to France, in his diary kept in Paris in 1779. His portrait, nearly full length, in the crimson velvet court dress in which he was presented to Louis XVI is in the possession of his grandson, the Bishop of California. He returned in 1784, conformed to the government and died at his place Greenvale Farm, near Poughkeepsie, in 1807.

II.

LAWRENCE.

The first ancestor of this family of whom we have any knowledge was Robert Laurens, Knight, of Ashton Hall, Lancashire, England. He accompanied Richard, Cœur de Lion in his famous crusade to Palestine, and distinguished himself at the siege of St. Jean d'Acre in 1191, by being the first to plant the banner of the Cross on the battlements of that town. For this he received the honors of knighthood from King Richard and also a coat of arms, with the fire cross (cross *raguly gules*), which is borne by his descendants to this day.[1] His family intermarried with that of the Washingtons, his grandson, Sir James Laurens, having married Matilda Washington in the reign of Henry III.

After this the family became eminent in England. Sir William Laurens, born in 1395, was killed in battle in France in 1455, with Lionel, Lord Welles. Sir John Law-

---

[1] *Holgate's Genealogies*, p. 201. It is impressed on the seal appended to the will of William Lawrence, 1680, and also to the will of Richard Lawrence, 1711, in the surrogate's office, New York city.

rence was one of the commanders of a wing of the English army at Flodden Field, under Lord Edward Howard, in 1513. Another Sir John Lawrence, the ninth in lineal descent from the above Sir Robert Laurens, possessed thirty-five manors, the revenue of which, in 1491, amounted to £6,000 sterling, *per annum*. Having however killed a gentleman usher of Henry VII, he was outlawed and died an exile in France, when Ashton Hall and his other estates passed, by royal decree, to his relatives Lord Monteagle and Lord Gerard.

Another member of this family was Henry Lawrence, one of the patentees of Connecticut in 1635, with Lord Say and Seal, Lord Brook, Sir Arthur Hasselrigg, Richard Saltonstall, George Fenwick and Henry Darley. They commissioned John Winthrop, Jr., as governor over this territory, with the following instructions: " To provide able men for making fortifications and building houses at the mouth of the Connecticut river and the harbor adjoining; first, for their present accommodation, and then such houses as may receive men of quality, which latter houses we would have builded within the fort." The patentees all intended to accompany Gov. Winthrop to America, but were prevented by a decree of Charles I.

This Henry Lawrence was in great distinction in England during Cromwell's time. Born in 1600, he became a Fellow Commoner of Emmanuel College, Cambridge, in 1622, but having taken the Puritan side, he was obliged to withdraw for a time to Holland. In 1641, he was Member of Parliament for Westmoreland, but when the life of the King was threatened, he withdrew from the Independents. In a curious old pamphlet, printed in the year 1660, entitled "The mystery of the good old cause, briefly unfolded in a catalogue of the members of the late Long Parliament, that held office both civil and military, contrary to the self-denying ordinance," is the following passage: "Henry Lawrence, a member of the Long Parliament, fell off at the murder of His Majesty; for which the Protector, with great zeal, declared that a neutral spirit was more to be abhorred than a Cavalier spirit, and that such men as he, were not fit to be used in such a day as that, when God was cutting down Kingship root and branch. Yet he came into play again, and contributed much to the setting up of the Protector; for which worthy service, he was made and continued Lord President of the Protector's Council, being also one of the Lords of the other House."[1]

He married Amy, daughter of Sir Edward Peyton, Bart., of Iselham in Cambridgeshire. He leased his estates at St. Ives, from the year 1631 to 1636, to Oliver Cromwell,

[1] *Harleian Miscellany*, vol. vi, p. 489.

to whom he was second cousin. He was twice returned as Member of Parliament for Hertfordshire, in 1653 and 1654, and once for Colchester borough in Essex, in 1656 : his son Henry representing Caernarvonshire, the same year. He was President of the Council in 1656, and gazetted as " Lord of the other house," in December, 1657. On the death of Cromwell, he proclaimed his son Richard as his successor. In *Thurloe's State Papers*, vol. II, is a letter to him from the Queen of Bohemia, (sister of King Charles), recommending Lord Craven to his good offices. From the tenor of this letter it appears that they were in the habit of corresponding. In a Harleian manuscript, No. 1460, there is a drawing of all the ensigns and trophies won in battle by Oliver, which is dedicated to his councillors and ornamented with their arms. Amongst these are those of Henry Lawrence, the Lord President, viz : a a cross, *raguly gules*, the crest, a fish's tail or demi-dolphin. A portrait of the President is inserted in *Clarendon's History of the Rebellion*. His monument, not yet effaced, is in the Chapel of St. Margaret's, *alias* Thele, in Hertfordshire.[1]

While the Dutch were prosecuting their settlements on Long Island and in New York, English settlers were also turning their attention to the same points. Among these

[1] *Holgate*, p. 262.

in 1635, were two brothers, John and William Lawrence who emigrated from Great St. Albans, Hertfordshire, England, and were shortly afterwards followed by their brother Thomas. They were cousins of the above named Henry Lawrence, being descended from John Lawrence, who died in 1538, and was buried in the Abbey of Ramsey.

They all became large landed proprietors and rose to eminence in the colony. John was one of the patentees of Hempstead on Long Island, under grant from the Dutch governor, Kieft, and also in 1645, one of the patentees of Flushing, on the same island. In 1663, we find him one of the Commissioners to settle the boundary line between New England and the Dutch colonies. In 1672, he was appointed Mayor of the city of New York, and in 1674, one of His Majesty's Council, in which office he continued, by successive appointments, till 1698. He was again appointed Mayor in 1691, and in 1692, Judge of the Supreme Court, in which office he remained till his death in 1699.

William Lawrence was also one of the patentees of Flushing, and his correspondence during the years 1642-3, with Gov. Stuyvesant, may be found among the archives at Albany. He was the largest landed proprietor at Flushing, a magistrate both under the Dutch and English government, and seems to have been a gentleman of affluence, as his sword, plate and personals alone were valued at £4,430 sterling.[1]   His widow, Elizabeth, subsequently married Sir Philip Carteret, Governor of New Jersey, and from her Elizabethtown received its name.

The other brother, Thomas, was the patentee of Newtown, Long Island, and the proprietor of the whole of Hell Gate Neck.   This Sir William was one of the " Committee of Safety " by whom the government of the colony was administered, and, soon after, one of the " Council of the Province," under a commission from Queen Anne, which office he held from 1702 to 1706.

In the next generation, Thomas, during the French war in 1758, was appointed, at the age of twenty-five, Captain of the Sloop of war Tartar, of eighteen guns, and later in life, was one of the Judges of Queen's county.   Another of the family, John Lawrence, married a daughter of Philip Livingston, sister of Gov. William Livingston of New Jersey.   He died in 1764, when the celebrated Whitfield, then in this country, preached his funeral sermon, and his body was deposited in the yard of Trinity Church, New York, in the family vault of his brother-in-law, the Earl of Stirling.[2]

---

[1] See inventory of his estate in surrogate's office, New York, in 1680.

[2] *Thompson's History of Long Island*, p. 427.

During the Revolution, this family was one of the few great landed families of New York which espoused the popular side. Many of its members were leaders in the contest. Jonathan Lawrence was, in addition to many other appointments, a member of the Provincial Congress which met in New York in 1775, and in 1776–7, a member of the Convention which formed the first Constitution of the State. He was also a Major in the Continental army. Another member of the family, Nathaniel, was Attorney-general of New York, in 1792–95.

In the last generation, the reputation of the family for patriotic gallantry was upheld by Captain James Lawrence, United States Navy, who fell in command of the frigate Chesapeake, in the action with the British frigate Shannon, June 1, 1813.

Isaac Lawrence, Esq., whose daughter married the RIGHT REV. DR. KIP, Bishop of California, was fifth in descent from Thomas Lawrence of St. Albans, mentioned above as one of the first of the family who came from England. He was President of the branch of the United States Bank in New York, until that institution was abolished by government. He died in 1841.

III.

VAN RENSSELAER.

The first ancestor of the family in America, De Heer Kiliaen Van Rensselaer, was the thirteenth descendant in a direct line from Henry Wolters Van Rensselaer of Nykirk in Guilderland, Netherland.[1] He was a Director in the Dutch West India Company and emigrated to America in 1637. Here he purchased from the Indians, it being afterwards confirmed by a grant of the government, a tract of country, twenty-four miles in length by forty-eight in breadth, comprising 700,000 acres. Through the centre runs the Hudson river.

This was erected by government into the Manor of Rensselaerwyck. It was "a form of feudal aristocracy transferred to American soil. The territory was made a manor with feudal appendages. The individual thus undertaking colonization, was designated, in the charter, as a Patroon, and endowed with baronial honors. He had, for example,

---

[1] *O'Callaghan's History of New Netherland*, vol. I, p. 122.

the prerogatives of sovereignty over the domain which he had thus acquired; administered the laws personally or by functionaries of his own appointment; appointed his own civil and military, as well as judiciary officers; and had magazines, fortifications and all the equipments of a feudal chieftain. His tenants owed him fealty and military service, as vassals; all adjudications in his court were final, with the exception of civil suits amounting to fifty guilders and upwards, when an appeal lay from the judgment of the Patroon to the Director General and Council. And it is probable that a similar remedy was also afforded in all criminal offenses affecting life and limb; this being one of the modifications already engrafted upon the feudal sovereignties of Europe."[1]

One of the family, Nicholas Van Rensselaer, was a minister of the Dutch Reformed Church, and being presented to Charles II, then an exile at Brussels, he prophesied the restoration of that monarch to the throne of England; which circumstance obtained for him afterwards a cordial reception at the court of St. James, when he visited London as chaplain to the Dutch embassy. In acknowledgment of the truth of the prediction, the king presented him with a snuff box, on the lid of which was set his majesty's

---

[1] *Holgate's Genealogies*, p. 29.

miniature.   This royal relic is still in the possession of the Van Rensselaer family at Albany.[1]

At the revolution of 1775, the proprietor of the Manor, Stephen Van Rensselaer, was a minor, and therefore excused from hazarding his wide domain by espousing either side in the contest. He married a daughter of Gen. Philip Schuyler, and besides other offices, was, in 1795, elected Lieutenant Governor of the state, John Jay being Governor.

Another of the family, Major General Solomon Van Rensselaer, was well known as the leader of the troops which stormed Queenstown Heights, Oct. 13, 1812, where he was dangerously wounded, having received six balls in his body.

At the close of the Revolution, the unoccupied parts of the Manor were laid out in farms of a hundred and fifty acres each.   Of these, nine hundred farms were leased by the Patroon between the years 1787 and 1798. At one time, he is said to have had, within the bounds of the Manor, five thousand tenants who voted. The marked feudal character of this tenure was too much at variance with the spirit of our institutions, producing combinations against the proprietor, known as the anti-rent war. The

[1] O'Callaghan's History of New Netherland, vol. I, p. 122.

late Patroon, therefore, in many cases, sold to the occupants the fee of their farms, so that the Manor has been greatly reduced.

The Manor House on the verge of Albany, erected in 1765, is still the residence of the family.

The Hon. John S. Van Rensselaer, whose daughter married LEONARD KIP, ESQ., of Albany, died in 1868. He was a descendant of the third Patroon, Jeremias, who died in 1674, and a son of Kilian K. Van Rensselaer, who represented Albany in Congress for five successive terms. Three of his uncles served in the Revolutionary war. Nicholas Van Rensselaer was Aid to General Schuyler, Philip was Quartermaster, and Henry K. a Colonel.

In the war of 1812, John S., though not yet of age, served as Aid on the Staff of Gen. Brown, Commander-in-chief of the United States Army, and rendered valuable services. He was Military Secretary and confidential Aid to Gov. DeWitt Clinton, during his administration, and in later life was appointed Judge of the county and Major General in the Militia of the State.